ARE YOU OKAY? SPORTS INJURIES

CAUSES, TYPES AND TREATMENT

Sports Book 4th Grade
Children's Sports & Outdoors

BABY PROFESSOR
EDUCATION KIDS

Sports injuries typically occur during exercise or participating in sports. Some happen by accident, but other can occur because of lack of conditioning, improper equipment, poor training practices, or insufficient stretching and warm-up. In this book, you will be learning about these injuries as well as what causes them and how to treat them.

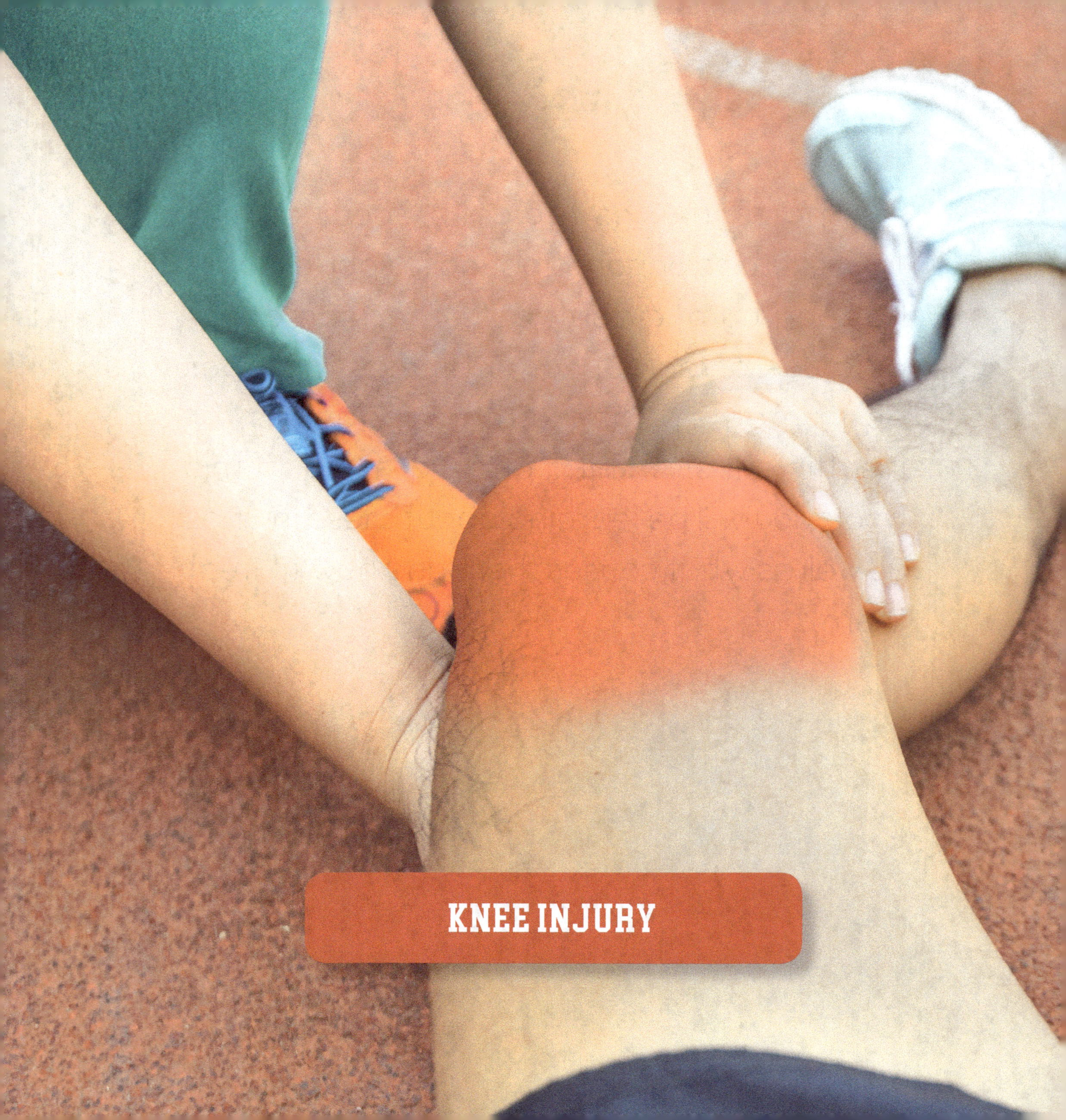
KNEE INJURY

Common sports injuries include dislocated joints, muscle strains and sprains, tears of tendons supporting the joints and allowing them to move, tears of ligaments holding the joints together, dislocated joints, and fractured bones, include the vertebrae.

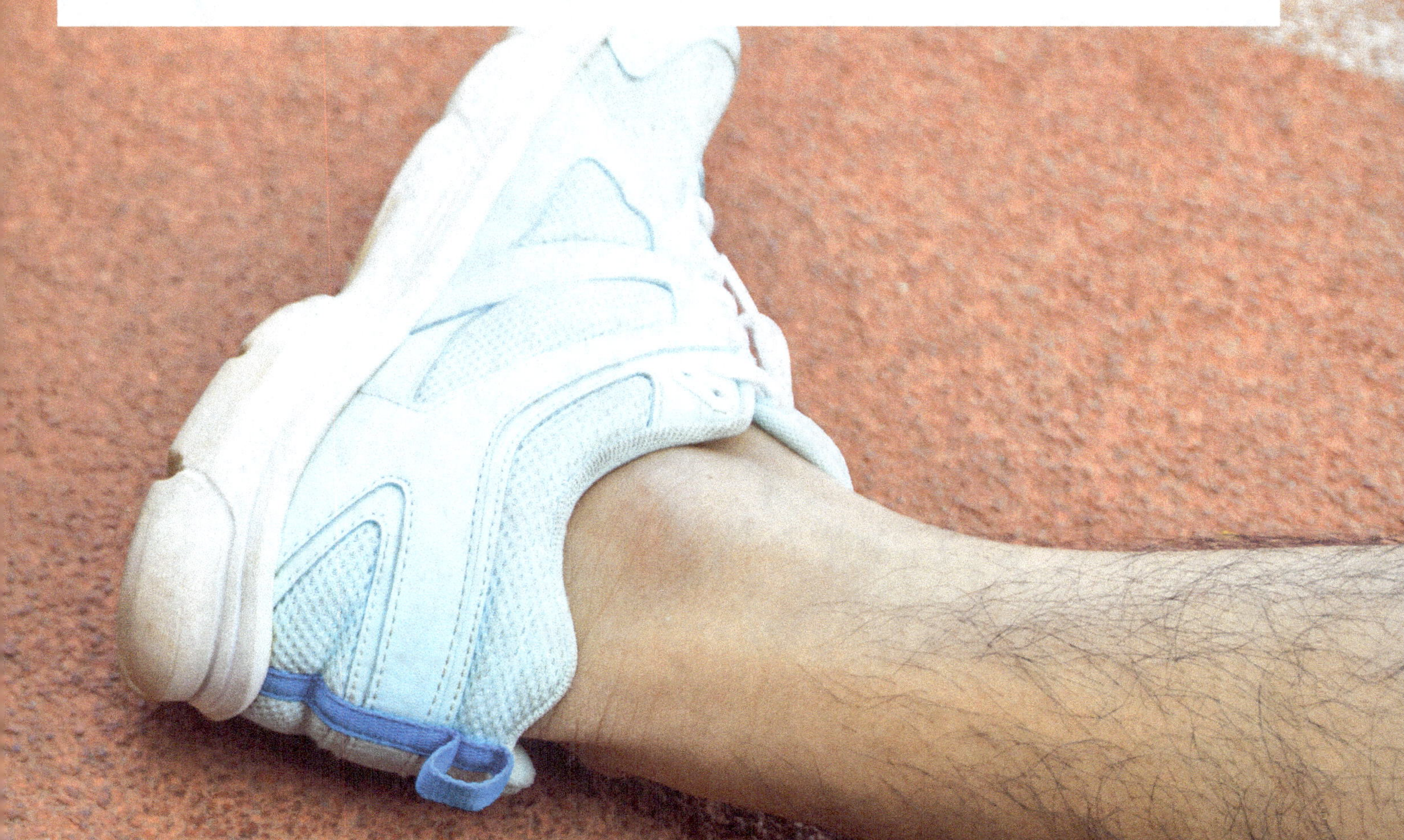

STRAINS AND SPRAINS

A strain is a tear, pull, or twist of a muscle or a tendon, which is the tissue that connects the muscle to the bone. A strain is an acute, noncontact type of injury resulting from over-contraction or over-stretching. Symptoms include loss of strength, muscle spasm, and pain. Even though it can be difficult to tell the difference between a mild and a moderate strain, if a severe strain is not professionally treated, it could result in damage as well as loss of function.

ATHLETE SUFFERING FROM
ANKLE INJURY

ANKLE SPRAIN

A sprain is a tear or stretch of a ligament, which is the band of connective tissues joining the end of one bone to another bone.

They typically occur from trauma such as a fall or a blow to the body knocking the joint out of position, and possibly rupturing the supporting ligaments.

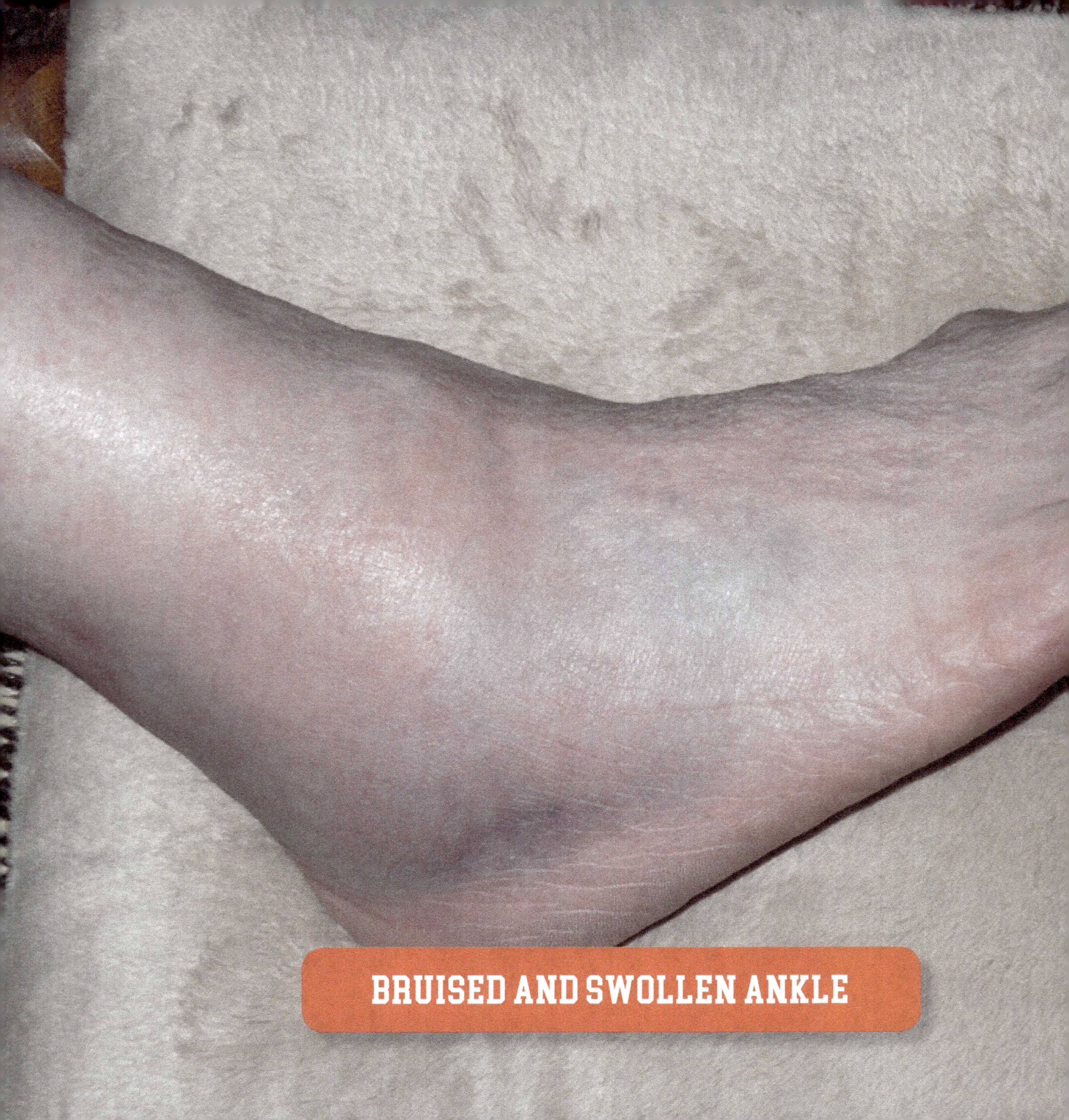
BRUISED AND SWOLLEN ANKLE

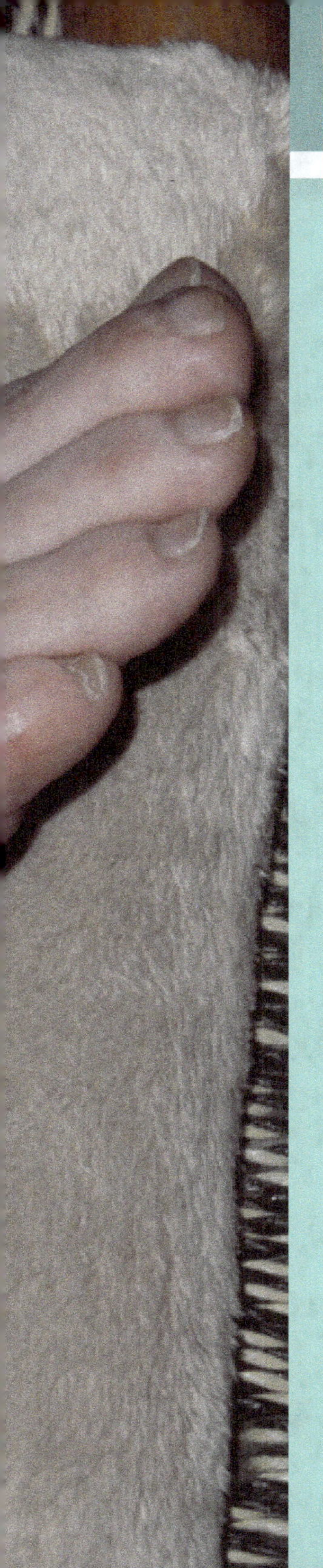

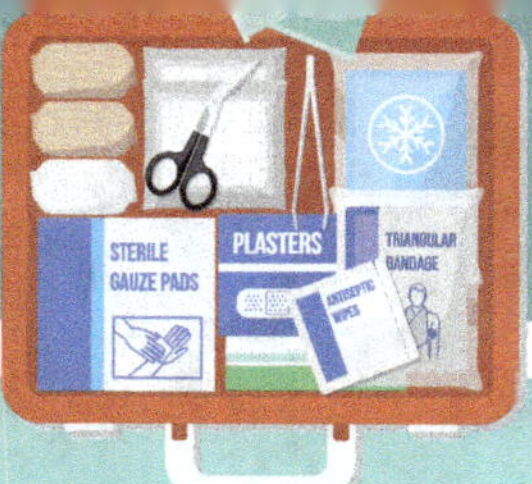

These can range anywhere from a first-degree sprain, which is a minimal stretch of the ligament, to a third-degree sprain, which is a complete tear of the ligament. The knees, ankles, and wrists are most vulnerable to this type of injury. Bruising, pain or tenderness, swelling, inflammation, inability to move the joint or limb, and instability are all signs of a sprain.

KNEE INJURIES

D ue to the complex structure of the knee as well as its weight-bearing capacity, it is a joint that is commonly injured. Knee injuries range from a mild injury to a severe injury. While still painful, some of the less severe injuries include runner's knee (tenderness and/or pain close or under the knee cap), iliotibial band syndrome (pain located on the knee's outer side), as well as tendinitis (degeneration of a tendon, typically where it meets the bone).

SOCCER PLAYER SUFFERING FROM
KNEE INJURY

Bruises to the bone or damage to the ligaments or cartilage are considered as more severe injuries.

njuries to the knees can be the result of a twist of the knee or a blow to the knee; taking an improper landing following a jump; or by running too much, too hard, or not warming up properly.

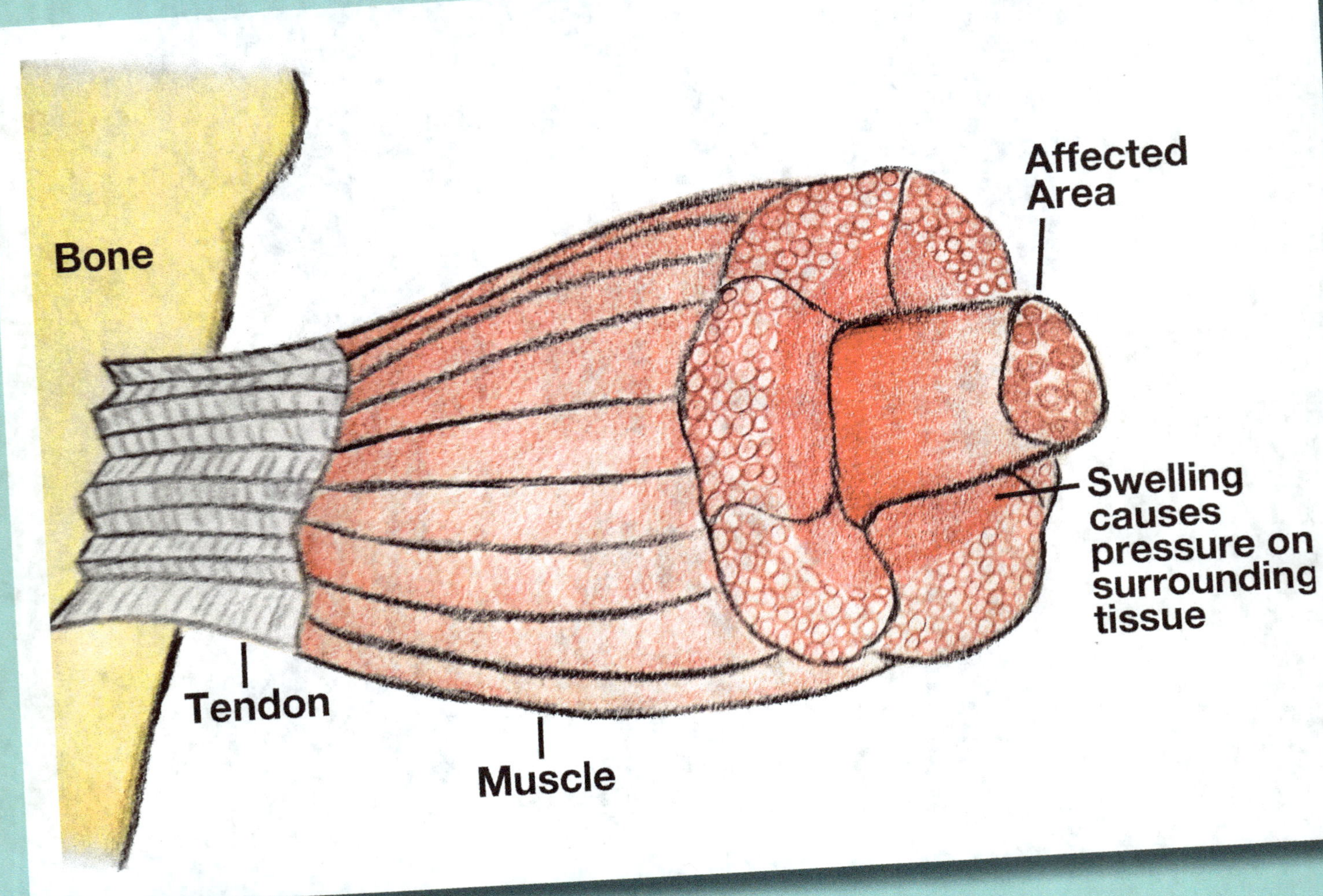

COMPARTMENT SYNDROME IN MUSCLE (CLEANED UP)

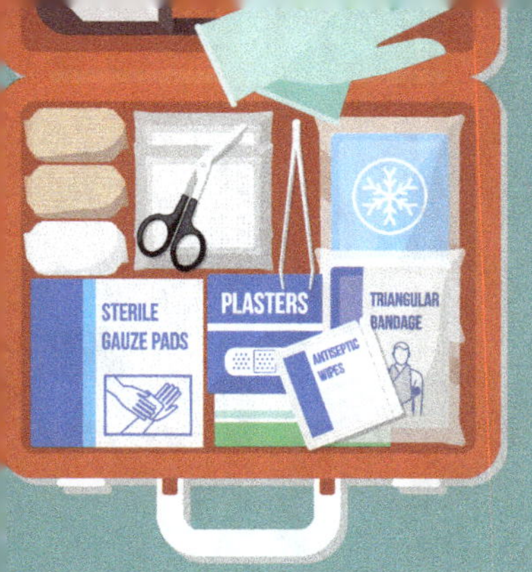

COMPARTMENT SYNDROME

Throughout the body, muscle (along with blood vessels and nerves running alongside and through them) are enclosed by a compartment that is formed by a tough membrane known as the fascia. Once muscles are swollen, they can fill this compartment to its capacity, which then causes interference with the blood vessels and nerves, causing damage to the muscles. This painful condition that results is known as compartment syndrome.

T his type of injury may result from a single traumatic injury (referred to as acute compartment syndrome), such as a hard hit to the thigh or a fractured bone, by repeated blows, or by constant overuse (referred to as chronic exertional compartment syndrome), which can occur in a sport such as running long-distances.

A WOMAN SUFFERING FROM
SHIN SPLINTS

SHIN SPLINTS

While the phrase "shin splints" has been used in describing any type of leg pain that is associated with exercise, it actually refers to the pain along the tibia (shin bone) which is the large bone located at the front of the lower leg. It can occur at the outside front part of the lower leg, include the ankle and foot, or towards the inner side of the bone where it joins the calf muscles.

Shin splints typically are seen primarily with runners, particularly some just beginning to run. Shin splint risk factors include incorrect use or overuse of the lower leg; improper warm-up, stretching, or exercise technique, jumping or running on hard surfaces, overtraining, or running in shoes not having good support.

MAN SUFFERING FROM BONE FRACTURES

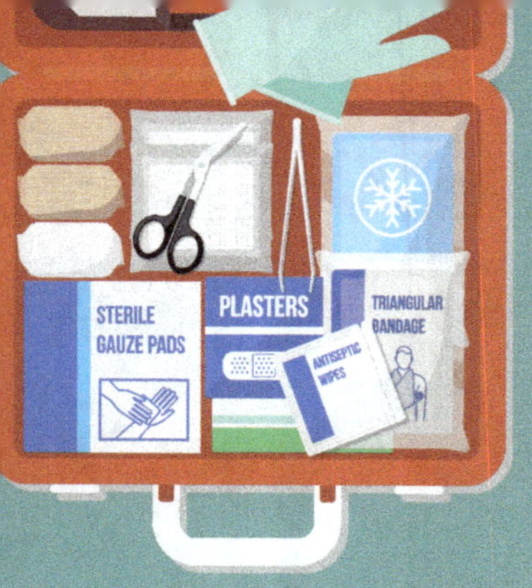

FRACTURES

Fractures are breaks to the bone occurring from either a one-time, quick injury to the bone (referred to as an acute fracture) or from repeated stress to that bone occurring over time (referred to as a stress fracture).

An acute fracture can be a simple fracture consisting of a clean break with a small amount of damage to surrounding tissue, or a compound fracture that consists of a break where a bone pierces through the skin and there is only a small amount of damage to surrounding tissue. Most of the time, an acute fracture should be considered to be an emergency. A fracture breaking the skin should be considered especially dangerous due to the risk of infection.

TYPES OF BONE FRACTURES

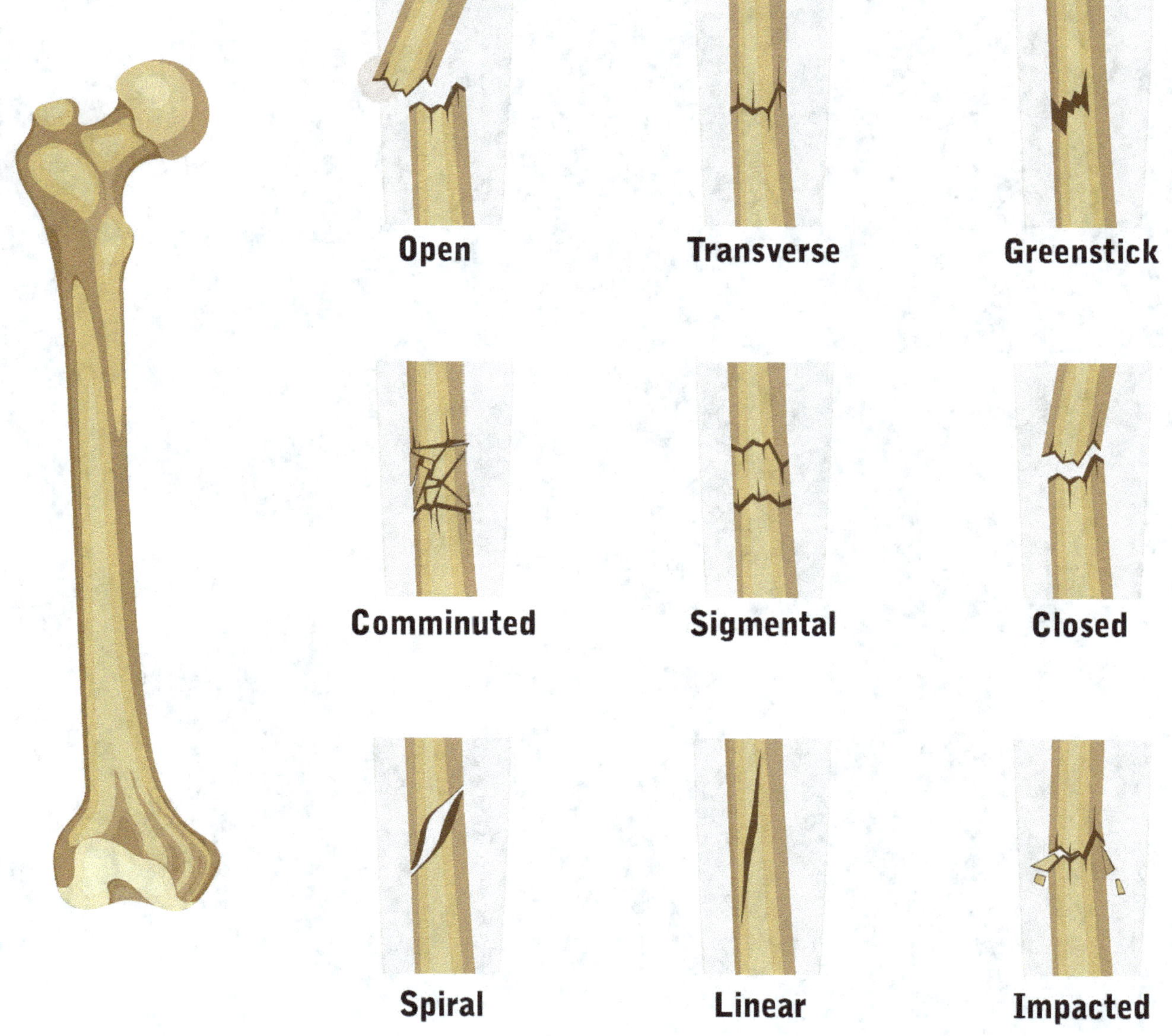

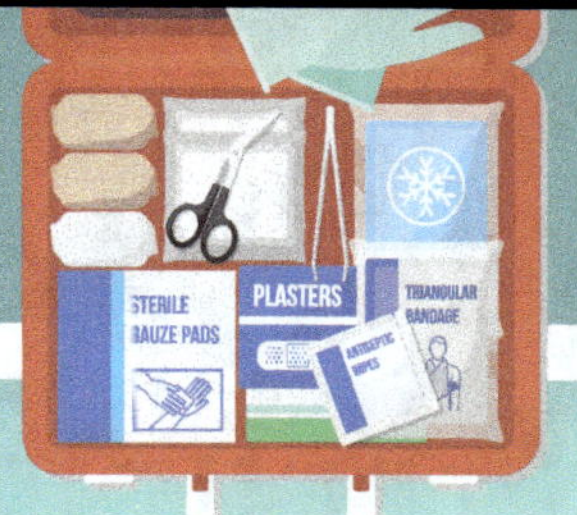

S tress fractures are fractures occurring mostly in the legs and feet and are most common in sports requiring repetitive impact, primarily running and jumping sports that include track and field and gymnastics. Running creates a force that is two or three times your body weight to your lower limbs.

DISLOCATIONS

A dislocation occurs when two bones that meet forming a joint have become separated. Most dislocations are the result of injuries sustained from contact sports including basketball and football, and high-impact sports as well as sports that result in excessive falling or stretching. This type of injury should be considered as an emergency requiring immediate medical treatment.

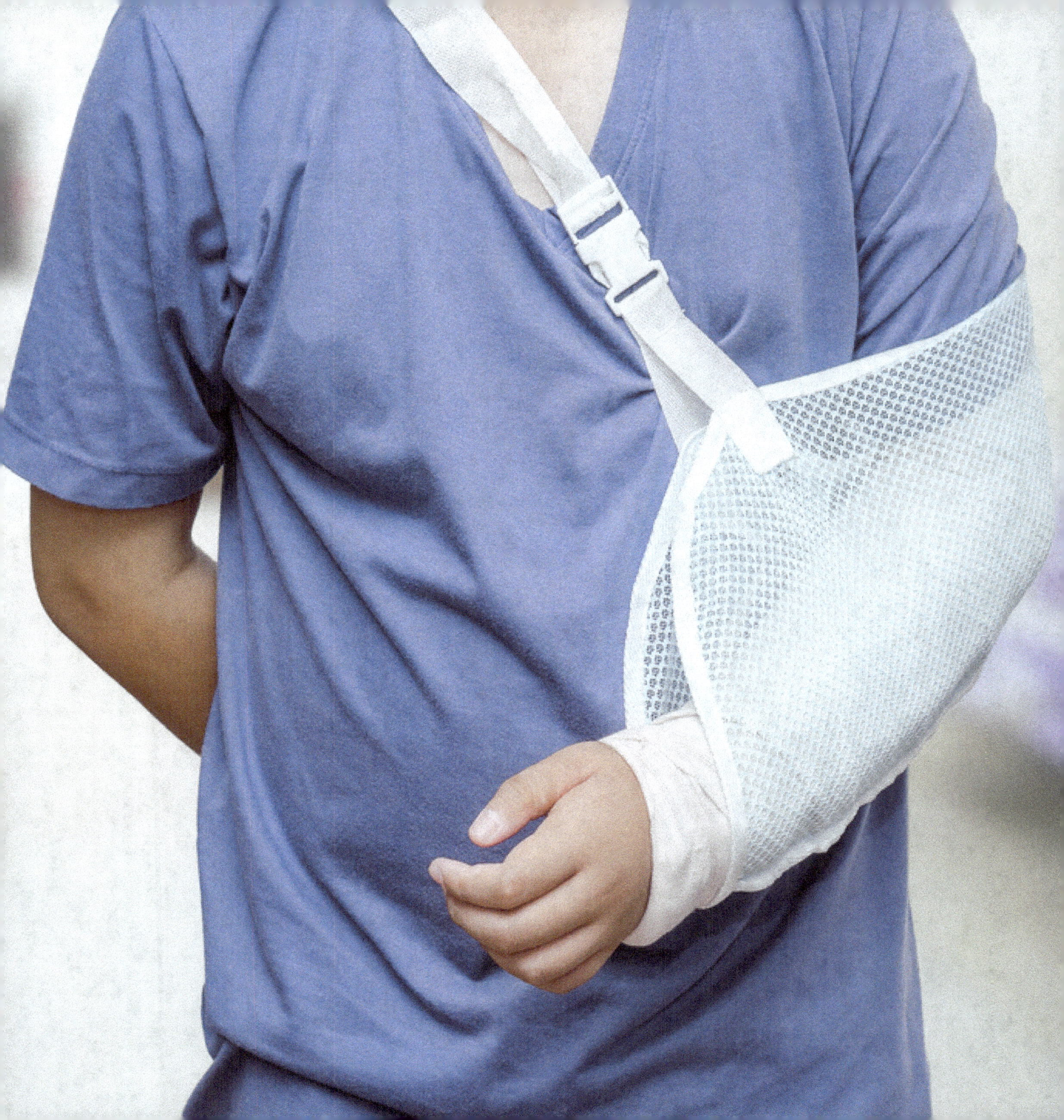

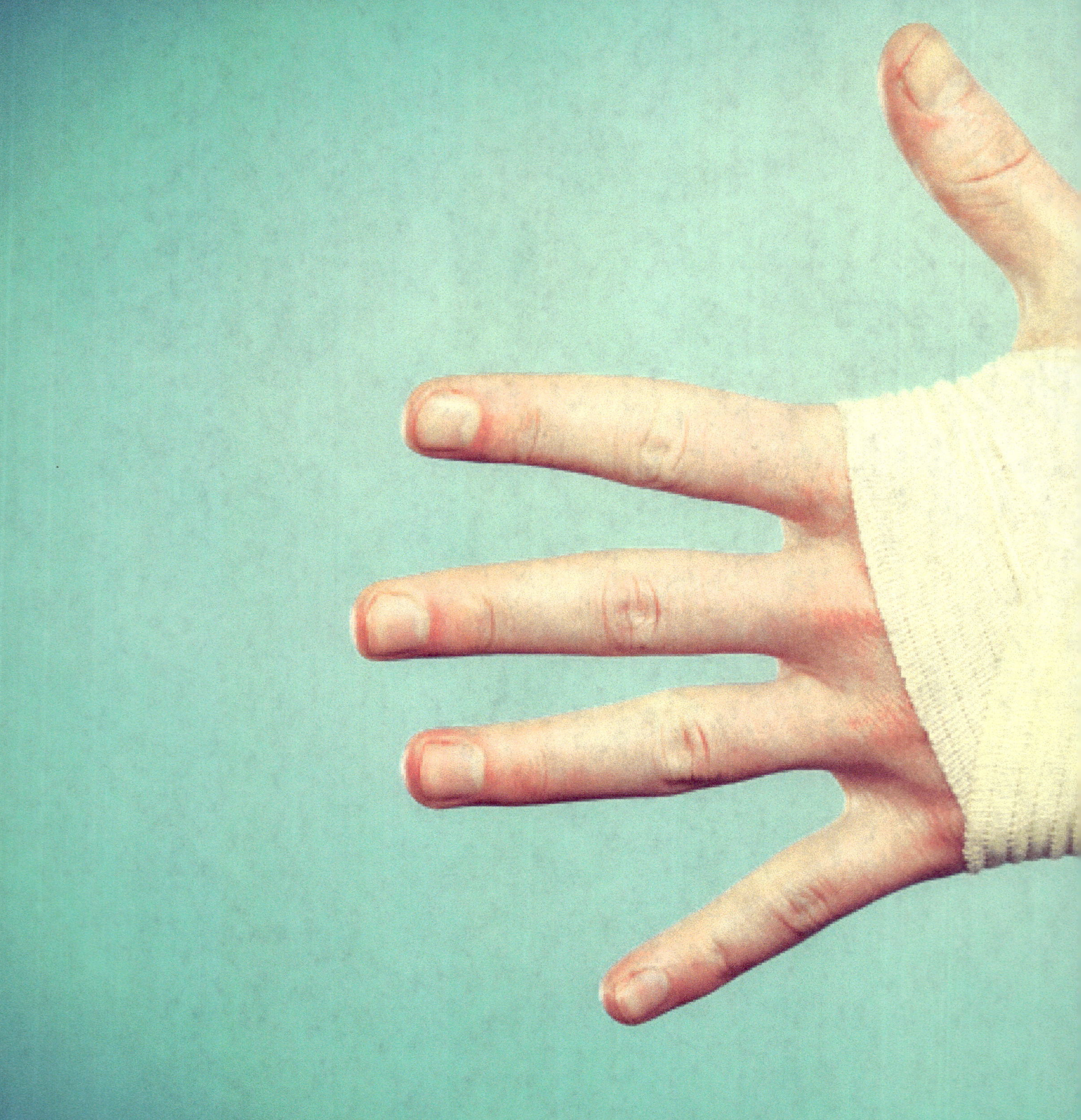

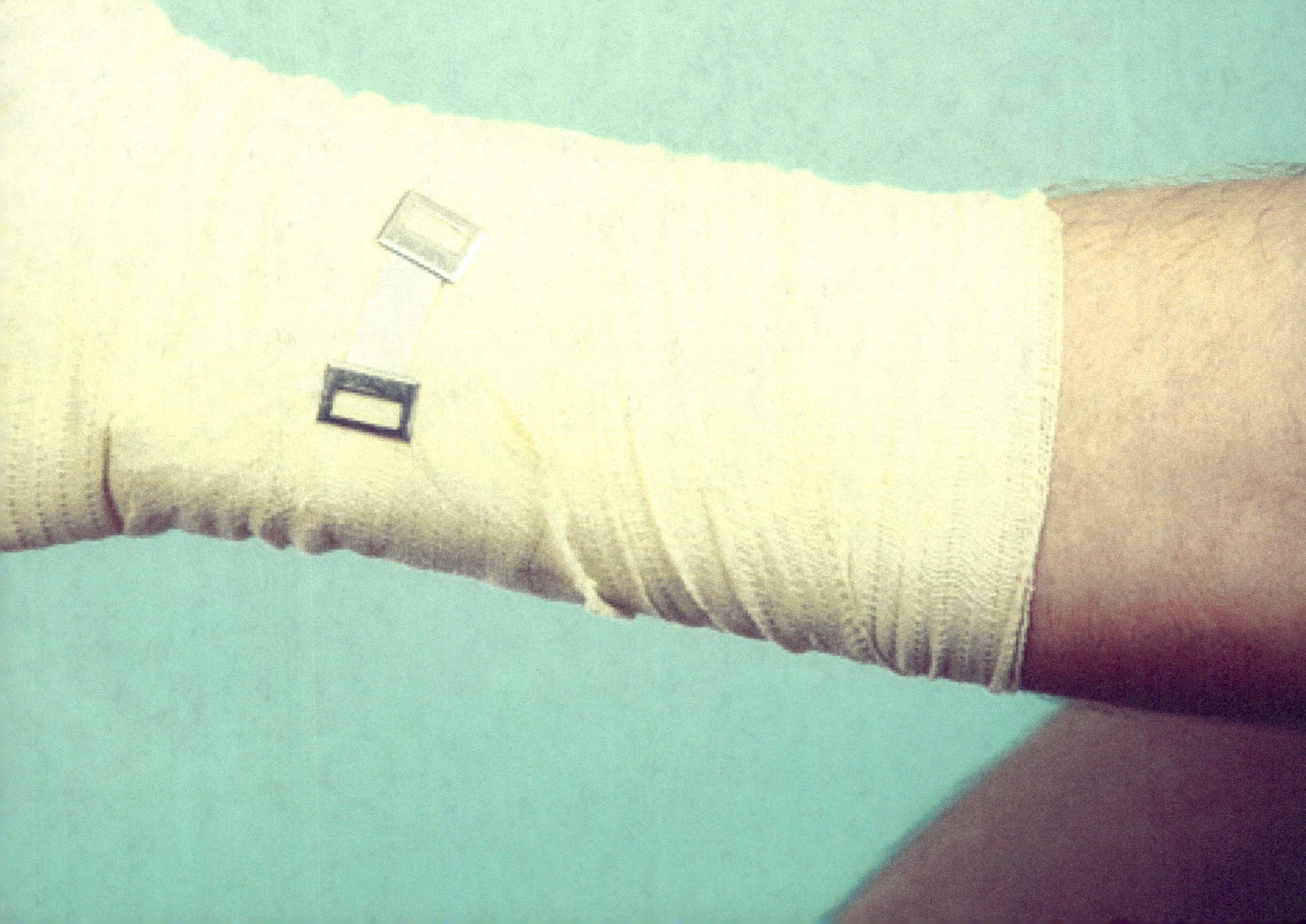

The hand joints are most likely to be dislocated, followed by the shoulder. It is uncommon for the elbows, hips or knees to sustain this type of injury.

ACUTE OR CHRONIC?

Musculoskeletal sports injuries are typically classified as either acute or chronic. Acute injuries typically occur suddenly during an activity and include a fractured hand, strained back, or sprained ankles.

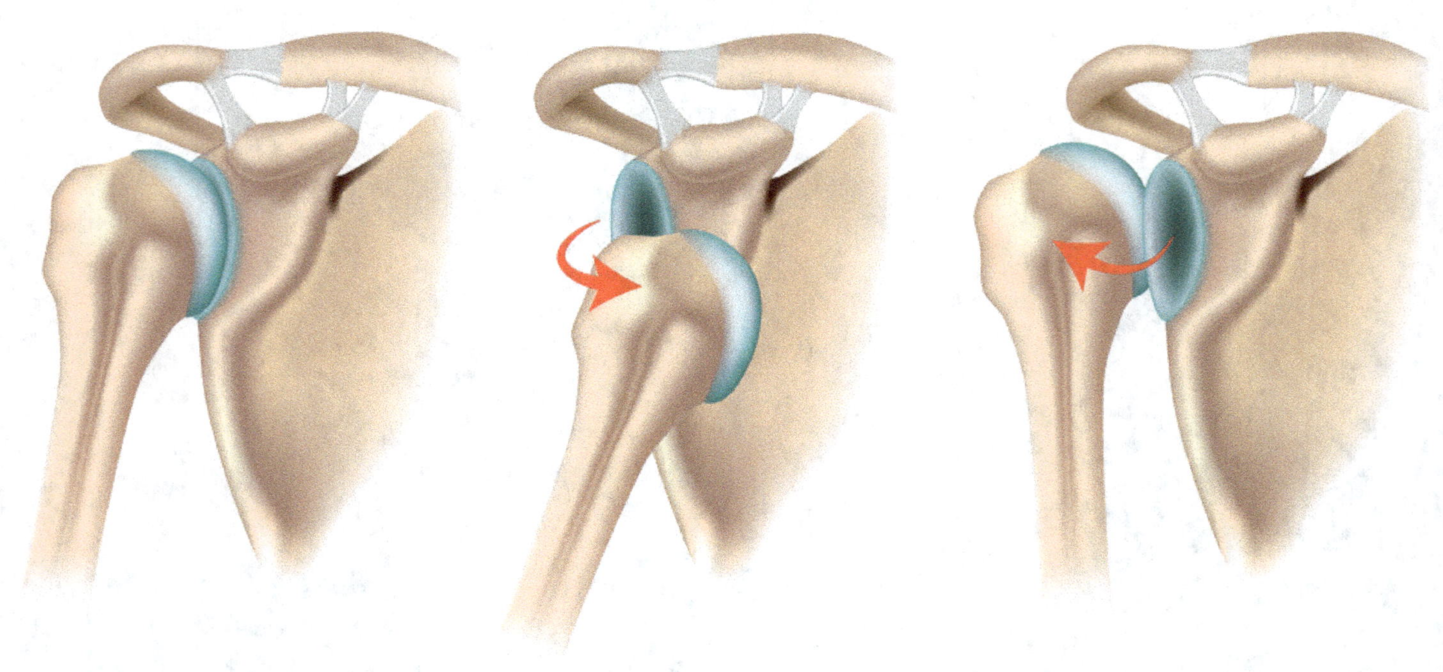

SHOULDER DISLOCATION

Signs that you might have an acute injury include a sudden, severe pain, inability to put weight on a lower limb, swelling, tenderness to an upper limb that seems to be extreme, unable to move the joint through a full range of motion, visible break or dislocation of the bone and extreme weakness to the limb.

C hronic injuries typically result from overuse of a certain area of the body when exercising or playing sports over a long period of time. Signs of a chronic injury include swelling, a dull ache when resting and pain when trying to do something.

WHAT SHOULD I DO WHEN I HAVE AN INJURY?

Whether it is an acute or chronic injury, you should never try "working through" its pain. If you experience pain from a certain activity or movement, STOP IMMEDIATELY! If you continue with the activity, you will only cause additional harm.

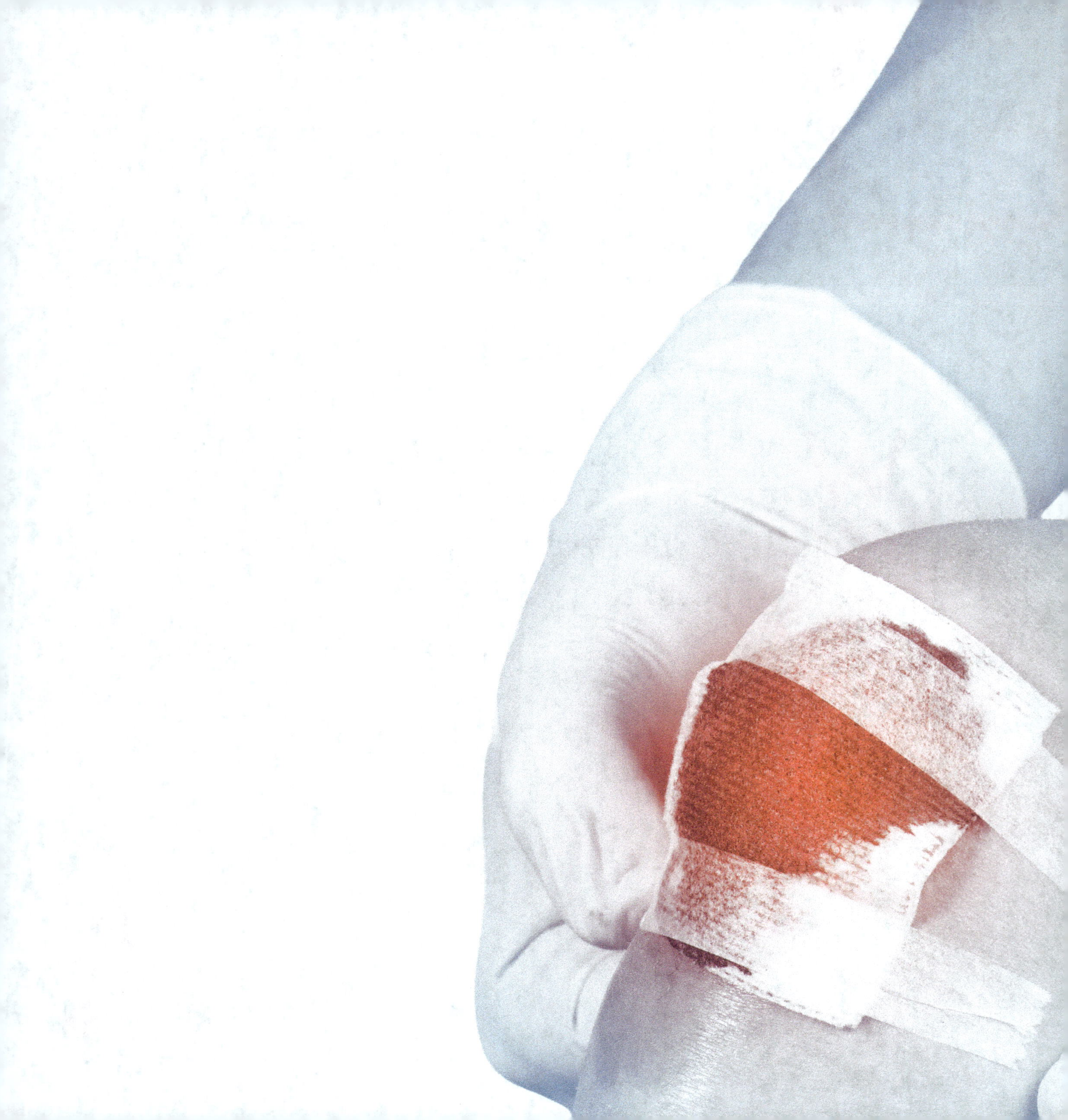

While some types of injuries will require immediate attention, others can possibly be self-treated.

You should contact a medical professional if your injury is causing severe pain, numbness, or swelling; you are unable to put any weight on the area of the injury or there is a dull ache or pain of a previous injury that is accompanied by additional swelling or joint instability or abnormality.

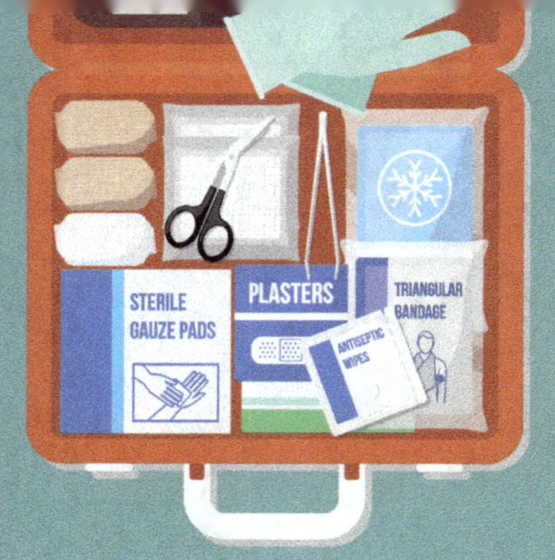

CAN MY INJURY BE TREATED AT HOME?

It is probably safe to treat your injury at home if you are not experiencing any of the symptoms mentioned above. However, if your pain or other symptoms get worse, you should probably have them checked out by your doctor.

1. REST
SPRAINED ANKLE
TREATMENT
2. ICE
3. COMPRESSION
4. ELEVATION

RICE METHOD

THE RICE METHOD

The RICE method can be used at home for relief of pain and inflammation and quick healing. Follow these steps immediately following your injury and continue at least 48 hours:

- REST
- ICE
- COMPRESSION
- ELEVATION

R EST: Reduce your regular activities and exercises as needed. If you are unable to put any weight on your knee or ankle, crutches might help. If you choose to utilize one crutch or cane for an ankle injury, be sure to use it on your uninjured side to help relieve weight on the ankle that is injured

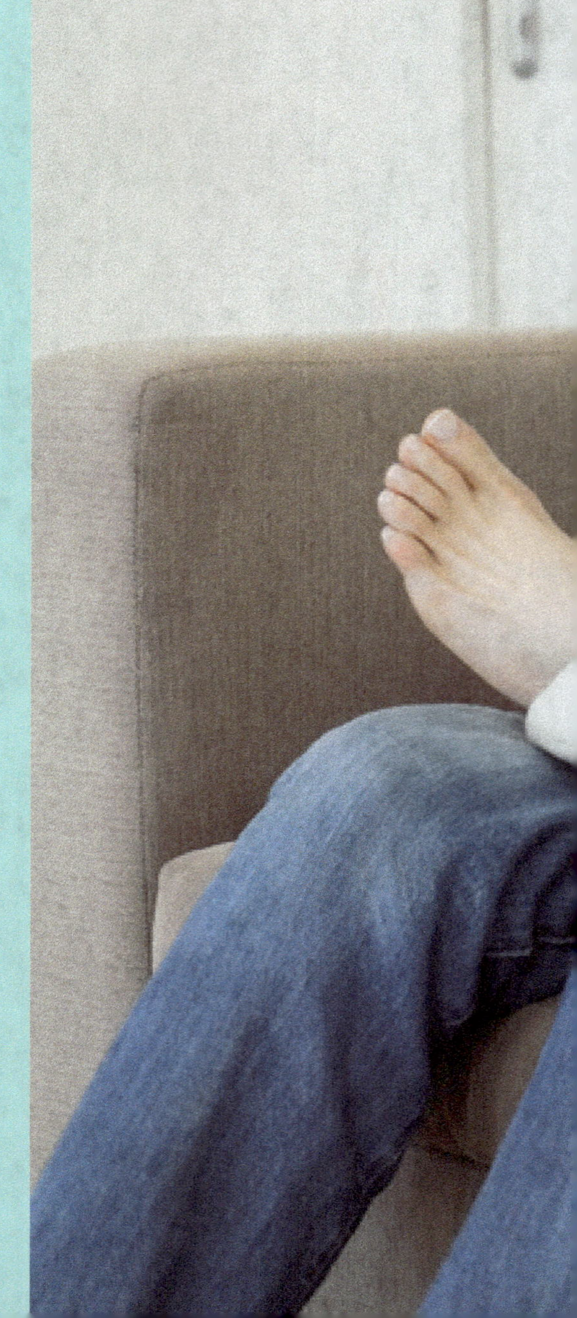

ICE: Be sure to apply ice to an injured area four to eight times a day, 20 minutes each time. To avoid frostbite, do not apply ice for longer than 20 minutes.

Don't use heat right after an injury since it can increase internal swelling or bleeding. You can use heat later to promote relaxation and relief of muscle tension.

COMPRESSION: Use compression on the area that is injured to help reduce swelling. You can use splints, air casts, special boots, and elastic wraps for compression. Ask your doctor which one you should be using.

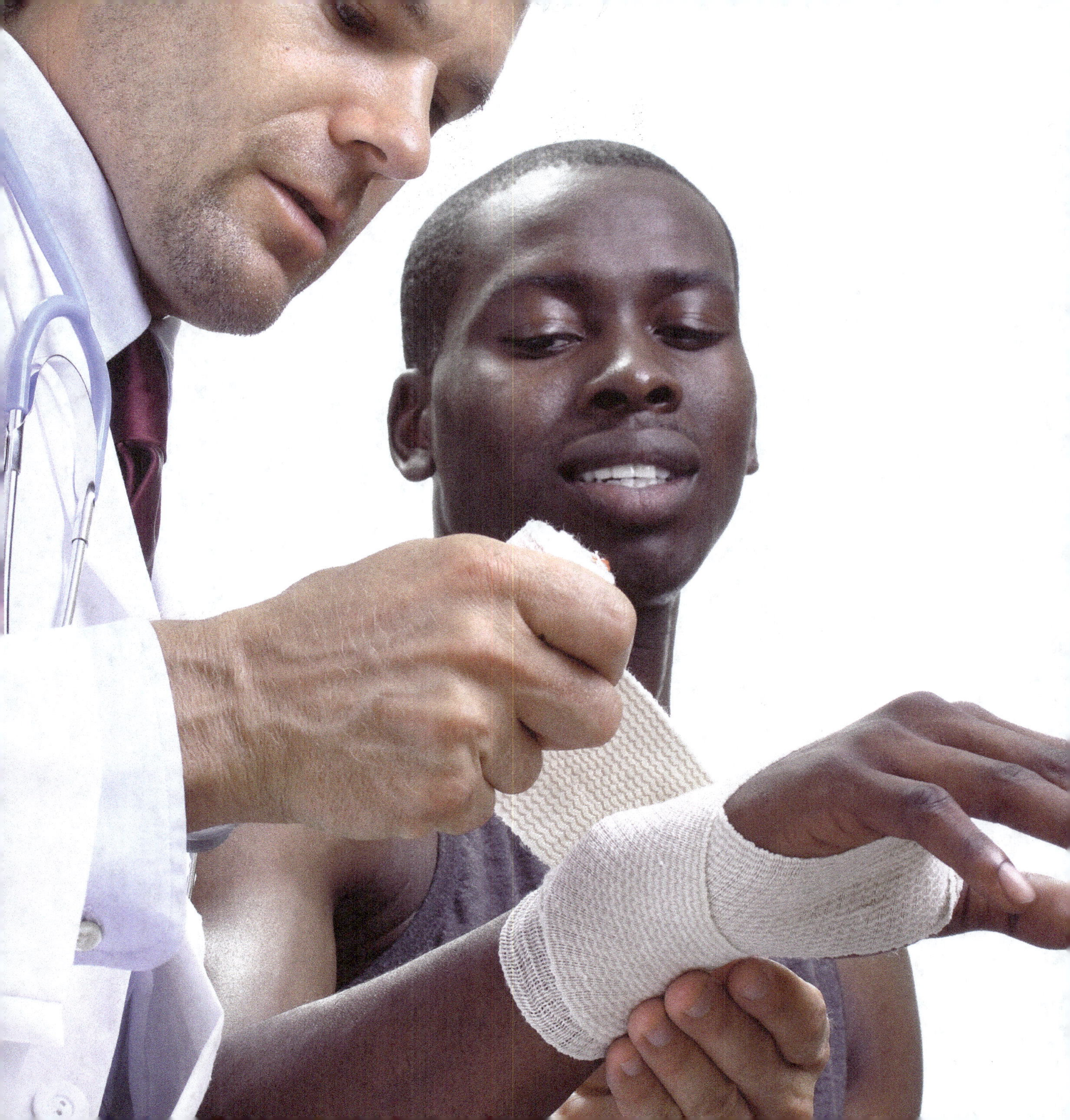

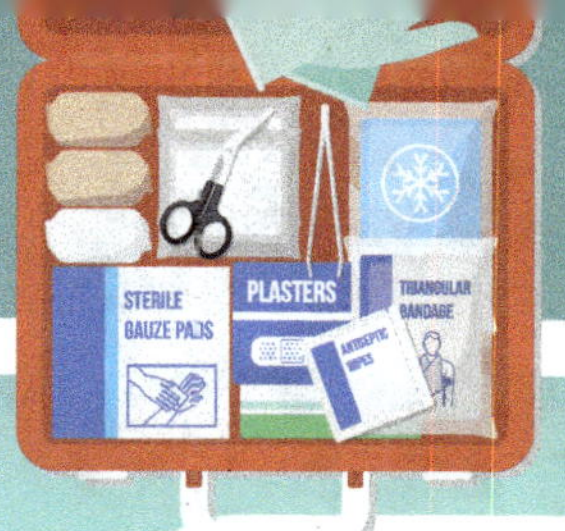

ELEVATION: Try to keep the injured knee, elbow, wrist, or ankle elevated on a pillow, above heart level. This will help to decrease swelling.

If you are unsure whether you should seek medical treatment, it is always a good idea to visit a health care professional for treatment.

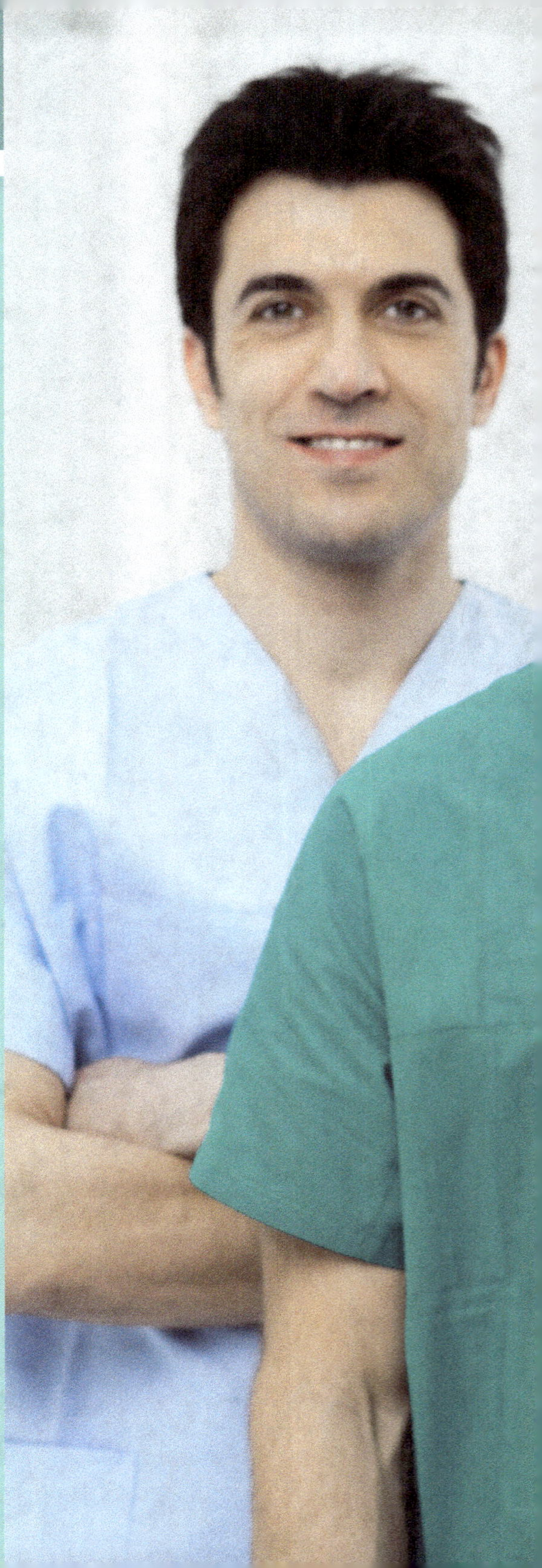

For additional information about sports injuries, how to prevent them, and how to treat them, you can visit your local library, research the internet, and ask questions of your teachers, family, and friends.

Visit

www.BabyProfessorBooks.com

to download Free Baby Professor eBooks
and view our catalog of new and exciting
Children's Books